SpringerBriefs in Electrical and Computer Engineering

For further volumes:
http://www.springer.com/series/10059

Nor Aziah Alias

ICT Development for Social and Rural Connectedness

 Springer

Nor Aziah Alias
Universiti Teknologi MARA
Shah Alam
Malaysia

ISSN 2191-8112   ISSN 2191-8120   (electronic)
ISBN 978-1-4614-6900-1   ISBN 978-1-4614-6901-8   (eBook)
DOI 10.1007/978-1-4614-6901-8
Springer New York Heidelberg Dordrecht London

Library of Congress Control Number: 2013932443

Printed on acid-free paper

Springer is part of Springer Science+Business Media (www.springer.com)

Preface

This book basically addresses ICT and connectedness in the context of rural community development. Of late, many authors put forward the capability of technology to provide a sense of connectedness that encompasses several facets including a sense of belonging, sharing, and a feeling of being touched. Synchronous and asynchronous communication media are primed to lead to a strong feeling of connectedness. Connectedness can be maintained and social networks can be accessed across geographical boundaries between people who may never have met.

It is the author's contention that ICT and connectedness may well be the topic of research and graduate courses in the near future. Since ICT has progressed tremendously in form and impact, the process of defining and refining *connectedness* as one of the psychological constructs tagged to it is pertinent. Moreover, due to its utilization in many contexts and fields, there exists substantial complexity, inconsistency, and lack of clarity in the conceptualization of connectedness. Thus, it is crucial that the term connectedness is defined within the context it is studied. What does connectedness via ICT really mean?

In addition, ICT for development (ICT4D) is fast becoming a discipline taught and researched by academics. In the context of rural communities, the physical presence of telecenters such as the Malaysian Rural Internet Centers (RIC) is in itself a platform to connect. Rural people meet at such centers to attend activities conducted by the center's personnel, thus giving them a chance to intensify existing relationships and collaborate on projects of common interest. Very few literatures have deliberated on ICT and connectedness in this context. An in-depth case of how ICT influences connectedness especially in relation to social and rural community development will thus be of benefit and interest to academics, NGOs, and governmental organizations alike.

Hence, the book is limited to introducing ICT in the context of rural connectedness. It deliberates on connectedness experienced by the users of rural Internet centers as they use ICT to perform their daily tasks and to be informed of events outside their community. The concept of connectedness in this case, embodies both social and online or electronic generated connectedness experienced by the rural community through access and accessibility to the Internet and government tools and services.

This brief consequently discusses the impact perceived by the RIC users and managers. The users' perspectives at the micro (community) level were considered. The approach is relevant for research on entities that tend to be local and particularistic such as the Malaysian RIC. Moreover, determining impact and causality of ICT in the rural community is an arduous task and requires a longitudinal investigation. Despite the limitations, the findings of a year's study of RIC users' connectedness highlighted various aspects of rural connectedness that are of value to researchers and other stakeholders.

It is the intent of this brief to incite an interest in ICT for development among researchers and developers alike. The rapid advances in ICT have been constantly enjoyed by the more affluent societies rather than those in isolated geographical locations. Technology must cease to divide. Technology is to bridge and connect people. Thus a thorough look at how ICT impacts the marginalized groups in rural areas is timely.

The brief is based on a research funded by IDRC (Canada) conducted in 2010. Data were collected through a paper and pencil survey, interviews, and online survey of managers and users of RIC in Malaysia.

In Chap. 1, an overview of connectedness is given. Chapter 2 outlines ICT for development (ICTD) and rural connectedness while Chap. 3 gives an account of rural connectedness via RIC in Malaysia. The reader is expected to gain a picture of connectedness through the utilization of ICT at such centers.

The author thank the project manager, advisors and team members of the Amy Mahan Research Fellowship Program for making the completion of this research possible.

Contents

Abbreviations

ICT   Information and Communication Technology
RIC   Rural Internet Center

Chapter 1
An Overview of Connectedness

This chapter discusses connectedness as a construct and how it is defined and explored in various fields. It will focus on the psycho- social dimension of connectedness and thus, will highlight the definition of connectedness from a psychological perspective. The chapter then briefly relates connectedness to existing theories including Self Determined Theory. Recent research on connectedness will also be highlighted to provide the rationale and to frame the research described in Chap. 3.

So, what is connectedness?

The word connected simply means "joined or linked together". Thus, one may refer to connectedness as a state of being joined or linked together.

Researchers who study connectedness view it in the light of several fields and contexts. Connectedness has been studied in fields such as psychology (Yoon and Lee 2010; Baumeister and Leary 1995; Russell et al. 2004), sociology (Romero et al. 2003), higher education (Glaser and Bingham 2008; Terrell et al. 2009), teacher education (Daves and Roberts 2010) and communication (Wei and Lo 2006, Gray and Dennis 2010). Research on connectedness extend over small group studies of family connectedness and adolescent connectedness to bigger realms such as the workplace, and academic connectedness. Timpone (1998) for instance, studied connectedness to society in relation to voters' turnout in an election while Scott (2009) studied factors of connectedness that lead to academic success of visually impaired undergraduates in an American university. The US Department of Health and Human Development pay meticulous attention to school connectedness as they acknowledge the relationship between school connectedness and educational outcomes; also as a protective factor from adolescent's adverse behavious (CDC, US Department of Health and Human Development, 2009). In fact the notion of adolescent connectedness is an aspect of connectedness that has been more thoroughly studied as compared to the others (Karcher 2001; Taylor-Seehafer et al. 2008; Markham et al. 2010). Connectedness to nature has also been explored by authors such as Gosling and Williams (2010) and Perrin and Benassi (2009).

N. A. Alias, *ICT Development for Social and Rural Connectedness*,
SpringerBriefs in Electrical and Computer Engineering,
DOI: 10.1007/978-1-4614-6901-8_1, © The Author(s) 2013

Professional connectedness (Reading 2010) and rural connectedness (Fourie, 2008) are also emerging as research interests among many.

Thus, it may be assumed that connectedness is fast becoming a research topic. This is especially true as people become more connected via technology tools. Before further deliberation on connectedness can be made, it is necessary to scrutinize on the term itself and present a definition relevant to the intent and content of this book.

1.1 Defining Connectedness

Due to its utilization in many contexts and fields, there exists substantial complexity, inconsistency, and lack of clarity in the conceptualization of connectedness (Barber 2005). Several concepts and terms emerge in the deliberation of connectedness. For instance, Barber and Schluterman (2008) identified three key concepts contributing to connectedness including relatedness which refers to the importance of youths' interpersonal connections to significant others. In an earlier literature Baumeister and Leary (1995) assumed relatedness needs are met when one feels connected to others, loves others, and feels loved and included by others.

Hemmingway Measure of Adolescent Connectedness as suggested by Karcher (2001) postulates three separate elements to a sense of connectedness namely participation and support, sense of belonging and sense of relatedness. These constructs are embedded within the composite scales of family connectedness, social connectedness and school connectedness. Sense of belonging as connectedness also prevails in the work of Hill (2006, 2009) and Vandermark (2007). The term connectedness has also been used in particular to a certain context such as school. The Division of Adolescent and School Health, US Center for Disease Control and Prevention for instance defines school connectedness as "the belief by students that adults and peers in the school care about their learning as well as about them as individuals" (Centers for Disease Control and Prevention, U.S. Department of Health and Human Services 2009). The division also reports four antecedents to school connectedness i.e., support (adult support), belonging to a positive peer group, commitment to education and environment. The myriads of descriptions and terms used warrants connectedness to be defined within the context it is studied. Nevertheless, common themes are present across the many facets of connectedness. What does connectedness really mean?

Barber (2005) contended that connectedness has been associated with (1) a feeling state (2) property of a system of relations (3) quality of a relationship, and (4) liking an environment among many others. Rovai (2002) defines connectedness as the "feeling of belonging and acceptance and the creation of bonding relationships". Despite the different contexts in which connectedness was and still being studied, several constructs are apparent. These are:

- The presence of a network, **community** or society (The network may initially be a very small personal network of two or three players)
- Access to and participation in the network, community or society

- Link or attachment to the network, community or society

To a deeper extent, it is commonly associated with

- Feelings of membership and belongingness and a feeling that one is part of a bigger structure. This may include perception of support.

Thus as stated earlier, connectedness in the context of this brief is defined as the

Feeling of belongingness, being linked to and related to a network, community or society in which one is a part of.

Sense of connectedness is therefore the sense of belonging, being linked to and related to. At this point, it is crucial to reiterate the context in which connectedness will be discussed in this brief i.e., the rural circumstance. A sense of oneness among rural community members characterizes rural connectedness. Evidently, Lambert (2010) found 71 % of her research participants believe that the farm land serves as that point of connectedness. The oneness of a rural community may be enhanced by a meeting point or a center as well.

The rural community context is somewhat unique due to their distinctiveness in terms of geographical location. Connectedness may not be limited to the experience at the individual or the rural community level. People may be also sense the connection to the leader or the larger society from which they are isolated from.

Having access to knowledge and having a sense of relatedness to what is happening outside the community thus denotes a sense of connectedness among rural folks who may be marginalized or missing out on many of the latest technology projects and initiatives. This will be termed as rural connectedness. The foregoing definition and the abovementioned context will thus, frame the rest of the discussion in this brief.

1.2 The Psycho-Social Dimension of Connectedness

There are several theories that are linked to connectedness; the Self Determination Theory (SDT) is one of them. Competence, autonomy and connectedness are the three elements of Self Determination Theory (SDT) that has been expansively used to provide the theoretical lenses for the study of motivation in the milieus of health, work, education, and development of less advantaged (Deci and Ryan, 2012; Korpelainen et al. 2010; Villeneuve and Karsenti 2005) These three innate psychological traits are often cited to account for the human tendencies

to engage interesting activities, to exercise capacities, to pursue connectedness in social groups, and to integrate intrapsychic and interpersonal experiences into a relative unity.

(Deci and Ryan, pp. 229)

The phrase "pursue connectedness in social groups" is apt when discussing connectedness and ICT use in the context of a community or social group. SDT explains the human orientation towards towards growth, development, and integrated functioning. Activity and optimal development are not processes that happen automatically but depend on the social environment (Kreijns et al. 2011). Herein lies the need to feel connected and valued by others and to experience a sense of belonging. Relatedness is commonly linked to the desire to feel connected to others.

ICT definitely supports this need. In addition, Techatassanasoontorn and Tanvisuth (2008) espouse SDT as an appropriate theory to explain ICT usage behaviour due to its element of self motivation that inadvertently affects behavioral outcomes. Basically SDT may lead one to understand the adoption and use of an ICT system (Korpelainen et al. 2010). The motivation to connected via ICT thus has a distinct psycho-social dimension.

1.2.1 Social Connectedness

Social connectedness basically refers to the relationship people have with others (The Social Report 2010). It illustrates the connection between people, both within their immediate social groups and within the wider community. Van Bel et al. (2009) define social connectedness as a short-term experience of belonging and relatedness, based on quantitative and qualitative social appraisals, and social awareness. They maintain two types of social connectedness:

> Social connectedness at the overall level pertains to one's whole social network, while social connectedness at the individual level is the feeling regarding a particular person.

Sense of sharing and involvement has also been identified by Van Bel et al. (2009) to be one of the dimensions of social connectedness. They maintained that social awareness, shared understandings, knowing each others' experiences, and feelings of closeness contribute to this sense of sharing and involvement. Social connectedness may be regarded as a higher level of connectedness as it involves sharing at the community level. To understand it, a thorough investigation of the lower level connectedness is needed. This will be further discussed in the next chapter.

Drawing from the work of Karcher, Barber, Rovai, Deci and Ryan, Vandermark, Van Bel and others mentioned in the earlier sections, a general framework encompassing three separate elements leading to a sense of connectedness is proposed in Fig. 1.1. The socio-psychological constructs that structure this framework appear more useful for studying connectedness at the community level rather than connectedness to a person. As noted previously, the community may go beyond the local community to include the state and the nation.

It is pertinent at this point to reiterate that it is not the intention of this brief to scrutinize the psychological notion of connectedness in depth. Rather the discussion is structured to support the working hypothesis that ICT augments connectedness.

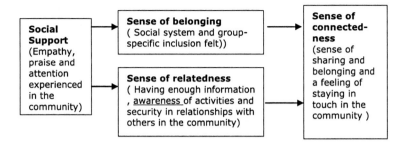

Fig. 1.1 A general framework of connectedness

1.3 Degree of Connectedness, Diversity of Connections and Platform to Connect

In order to make the most of the general framework for connectedness in the context of this brief, deliberation on several aspects of connectedness is imminent. The discussion that ensues will explore the degree of connectedness, the diversity of connections, and the mode or platform through which people are connected.

1.3.1 Level or Degree of Connectedness

The literature on connectedness is pervaded with the notion of intensity and degree of connectedness. Authors in the area of computer network refer to the number of links/ties as the indicator for degree of connectedness (Barolli et al. 2009) while others in the social sciences recognizes it as the level of intensity at which one is connected. Connectedness at its minimum does not require an immediate interaction between individuals. As a communication and sharing tool, blogs are increasingly being developed and read in today's society. Baumer et al. (2008) in their study on blog readers reported that participants felt that they were a part of a blog even though their presence were not known to the blog owners. Connectedness as described by the participants does not always mean feeling connected to the blogger as a person; some may read blogs because of the information presented. Awareness of presence has also been associated with connectedness (Moebs and McManis 2008). Similarly, IJsselsteijn et al. (2003) express connectedness as keeping up-to-date with other people's lives. On another level, Rettie (2003), indicates that receiving a text message may evoke the experience of connectedness. She suggests that connectedness is an emotional experience, evoked by, but independent of, the other's presence. In addition, Baumer et al. (2008) discovered that the participants may have started reading blogs for information purposes, but continued reading because they developed a connection with the blogger. They concluded that by being a part of a blog involves regular reading, a feeling of community, and a sense of connectedness. Thus, connectedness may extend from impression of connectedness to true connectedness. The degree of connectedness may vary between co-presence, an awareness of others, co-location, the feeling of being in the same place as others and the feeling of having someone else for support within reach (Biocca et al. 2003). As stipulated by Deci and Ryan 2000), a higher degree of connectedness lies in more than either a need for affiliation or a need for attachment. There is the need for regular social contact with those to whom one feels connected.

Alhir (2010) put forward three degrees of connectedness :

> The first degree of connectedness, *communication*, involves individuals informing one another.
> The second degree of connectedness, *conversation*, involves individuals conversing or dialoging with one another.
> The third degree of connectedness, *collaboration*, involves individuals co-creating together
> (Alhir 2010)

Alhir (2010)'s degrees of connectedness are very much related to social connectedness discussed beforehand.

1.3.2 Diversity of Connection and Degree of Proximity

Another dimension to be considered when discussing connectedness is the *diversity of connection*. This includes the different types of people, units, information, viewpoints, technologies that people can access in their network (Hansen 2009). Discussions on connectedness have also dwelled on the *degrees of proximity* to the individual (Barber 2005). Connectedness is possible between the individuals to (1) other individuals (parent, friend) (2) groups (e.g., family, peers) (3) institutions (e.g., schools) (4) society and (5) values (e.g., moral, spiritual).

1.3.3 Platform to Connect

Several means serve as points of connections and avenues for people to connect. These may be physical location, correspondence, the online realm or via other media. In the context of the rural communities, the physical presence of tele-centers such as the Malaysian RICs is in itself a platform to connect. Rural people meet at such tele-centers to attend activities conducted by the infomediary or center personnel, thus giving them a chance to intensify existing relationships and collaborate on projects of common interest. Such degree of proximity is also inherent in the online sphere.

This chapter has thus far, given a brief overview of connectedness and the different aspects related to its definitions, dimensions, degree, and platform to connect. In summary, connectedness rings with belongingness, being linked to and relatedness; it has a psycho-social dimension and may exist at different degrees.

Its definition varies slightly depending on the different context of its use. ICT as a platform to connect remains the mainstay of this brief. The subsequent chapter will address connectedness and ICT.

References

Alhir Si (2010) Degree of connectedness: Communication, conversation and collaboration. http ://salhir.wordpress.com/2010/05/24/degrees-of-connectedness-communication-conversation-and%C2%A0collaboration/. Accessed 10 Jan 2011

Barber BK (2005) Whence connectedness, hence connectedness, paper presented at the meeting on connectedness and adolescent health and development, National Research Council/ Institute of Medicine Board on children, youth, and families committee on adolescent health and development. http://www.bocyf.org/barber_paper.pdf. Accessed 15 Mar 2010.

Barber BK, Schluterman JM (2008) Connectedness in the lives of children and adolescents: A call for greater conceptual clarity. J Adolesc Health 43:209–216

Barolli L, Mino G, Xhafa F, De Marco G, Durresi A, Koyama A (2009) Analysis of Ad-Hoc networks connectivity considering shadowing radio model. Proceedings of the 7th international conference on advances in mobile computing and multimedia, pp 464–468, doi: 10.1145/1821748.1821836

Baumeister RF, Leary MR (1995) The need to belong: desire for interpersonal attachments as a fundamental human motivation. Psychol Bull 117:497–529

Baumer E, Sueyoshi M, Tomlinson B (2008) Exploring the role of the reader in the activity of blogging. Proceeding of the twenty-sixth annual SIGCHI conference on Human factors in computing systems, pp 1111–1120

Biocca F, Burgoon JK, Harms C, Stoner M (2003) Criteria and scope conditions for a theory and measure of social presence. Presence: Teleoperators Virtual Environ 12(5):456–480

Centers for Disease Control and Prevention (2009) School connectedness: strategies for increasing protective factors among youth. U.S. Department of Health and Human Services, Atlanta, GA

Daves DP, Roberts JG (2010) Online teacher education programs: social connectedness and the learning experience. J Instr Pedagog. http://www.aabri.com/jip.html. Accessed 11 Jan 2011

Deci EL, Ryan R (2000) The "what" and "why" of goal pursuits: human needs and the self-determination of behavior. Psychol Inq 11(4):227–268

Deci EL, Ryan R (2012) Self-determination theory in health care and its relations to motivational interviewing: A few comments. Inter J Behav Nutri Phys Act 9:24. doi:10.1186/1479-5868-9-24

Fourie L (2008) Enhancing the livelihoods of the rural poor through ICT: a knowledge map. InfoDev Working Paper 13, South Africa country study

Glaser HF, Bingham S (2008) Students' perceptions of their connectedness in the community college basic public speaking course. Paper presented at the annual meeting of the NCA 94th annual convention, TBA, San Diego, Online. http://www.allacademic.com/meta/p257700_index.html. Accessed 12 Oct 2009

Gosling E, Williams K (2010) Connectedness to nature, place attachment and conservation behaviour: Testing connectedness theory among farmers. J Environ Psychol 30(3):298–304

Gray D, Dennis D (2010) Audience satisfaction with television drama. University of Canterbury, Christchurch, New Zealand

Hansen MT (2009) Collaboration: how leaders avoid the traps, create unity and reap big results. Harvard Business School Publishing, Massachussetts

Hill DL (2006) Sense of belonging as connectedness, American Indian worldview, and mental health. Arch Psychiatry Nurs 20(5):210–216

Hill DL (2009) Relationship between sense of belonging as connected ness and suicide in American Indians. Arch Psychiatr Nurs 23(1):65–74

IJsselsteijn WA, van Baren J, van Lanen F (2003) Staying in touch: social presence and connectedness through synchronous and asynchronous communication media. In: Stephanidis C, Jacko J (eds) Human–Computer interaction: theory and practice (Part II). Proceedings of HCI International, vol. 2. pp 924–928

Karcher M (2001) The Hemingway: measure of adolescent connectedness— validation studies, Paper presented at the 109th annual conference of the American psychological association, San Francisco, 24–28 Aug 2001. Eric document number ED477969

Korpelainen E, Vartiainen M, Kira Mari (2010) Self-determined adoption of an ICT system in a work organization. J Organ End User Comput 22(4):51–69. doi:10.4018/joeuc.2010100103

Kreijns K, Vermeulen M, Van Buuren H, Van Acker F (2011) Wikiwijs and teachers' use of digital learning materials: self-determination theory and the integrative model for behavior prediction. Paper presented at the 38th Onderwijs Research Dagen (ORD), Maastricht, 8–10 June

Lambert DA (2010) Exploring the educational aspirations of rural youth: an image-based study using participant produced photographs. Unpublished doctoral dissertation, Colorado State University

Markham CM, Lormand D, Gloppen KM, Peskin MF, Flores B, Low B, House L (2010) Connectedness as a predictor of sexual and reproductive health. J Adolesc Health 46:23–42

Moebs S, McManis J (2008) Adaptive social connectedness in a multimedia e-learning environment. China-Ireland international conference on information and communications technologies. China IET Conference Publications, Beijing, pp 781–785

Perrin JL, Benassi VA (2009) The connectedness to nature scale: a measure of emotional connection to nature? J Environ Psychol 29(4):434–440

Reading C (2010) Using ICT to increase professional connectedness for teachers in remote Australia. Aust Educ Comput 25(2):3–6

Rettie R (2003) Connectedness, awareness and social presence, 6th international presence workshop, Aalborg. http://www.kingston.ac.uk/~ku03468/includes/docs/Connectedness,%20 Awareness%20and%20Social%20Presence.pdf

Romero N, Van Baren J, Markopoulos P, de Ruyter B, IJsselsteijn W (2003) Addressing interpersonal communication needs through ubiquitous connectivity: home and away. Lect Notes Comput Sci 2875:419–429

Rovai A (2002) Development of an instrument to measure classroom community. Internet High Educ 5(3):197–211

Russell CA, Norman AT, Heckler S (2004) The consumption of television programming: development and validation of the connectedness scale. J Consum Res 31(1):150–161

Scott R (2009) Undergraduate educational experiences: the academic success of college students with blindness and visual impairments. Unpublished doctoral dissertation, North Carolina State University

Taylor-Seehafer M, Jakobvitz D, Steiker LH (2008) Social connectedness and substance use in a sample of older homeless adolescents: preliminary findings, patterns of attachment organization. Fam Community Health 31(1):S81–S88

Techatassanasoontorn AA, Tanvisuth A (2008) The integrated self-determination and self-efficacy theories of ICT training and use: the case of the socio-economically disadvantaged. http://www.globdev.org/files/23-Paper-Techat-Integrated%20Self%20Determ.pdf. Accessed 8 Nov 2012

Terrell S, Snyder M, Dringus LP (2009) The development, validation, and application of the doctoral student. Internet High Educ 12(2009):112–116

The Social Report (2010) New Zealand ministry of social development. www.socialreport.msd. govt.nz/social-connectedness. Accessed 15 June 2010

Timpone RJ (1998) Structure, behaviour and voter turnout in the United States. Am Polit Sci Rev 92(1):145–158

US Department of Health and Human Services (2009)

Van Bel D, Smolders K, IJsselsteijn W, De Kort Y (2009) Social connectedness: concept and measurement. In: Kameas A, Reyes A, Royo D, Weber M, Callaghan V (eds) Proceedings of the 5th international conference on international conferences on intelligence environments, IOS Press, Armsterdam, pp 67-74

Vandemark LM (2007) Promoting the sense of self, place, and belonging in displaced persons: the example of homelessness. Arch Psychiatry Nurs 21(5):241–248

Villeneuve S, Karsenti T (2005) What are the factors related to the successful use of ICTs by student-teachers at the elementary-school Level? In: Kommers P, Richards G (eds) Proceedings of world conference on educational multimedia, hypermedia and telecommunications 2005, AACE, Chesapeake, USA, pp 2726–2731

Wei R, Lo V (2006) Staying connected while on the move: cell phone use and social connectedness. N Media Soc 8(1):53–72

Yoon E, Lee R (2010) Importance of social connectedness as a moderator in Korean immigrants' subjective well-being. Asian Am J Psychol 1(2):93–105

Chapter 2
ICTD and Rural Connectedness

This chapter illustrates how ICT influences connectedness in several realms particularly in education and community development. The chapter initially gives an introduction to ICT for development (ICTD) and description of how ICT has been utilized for rural community development. It will review relevant ICTD research and describe the different theories of change utilized by the researchers. This chapter ends with a general account of ICT and rural connectedness.

2.1 ICT for Development (ICTD)

Information and communication technology (ICT) is a term used to encompass all forms of computing systems, telecommunications and networks. In this brief, it is electronic means of capturing, processing, storing and disseminating information. Though the focus is on internet based technology, other communication tools such as radio and televisions are not to be dismissed as ICT tools as well.

ICT has infiltrated every nooks and corners of our lives. People are connected by ICT in many ways, spawning networks of information exchange, knowledge creation and community sharing. The ability to generate social connections resides in the multitude of social media applications, accessible via desktops, laptops, tablets, mobiles and handheld smart gadgets. The capacity to learn at a distance, at any time or anywhere has also been made possible via ICT.

ICT for development (ICTD or ICT4D) relates to the use of Information and Communication Technology (ICT) to support the development of people and communities in developing nations and underserved regions. It is fast becoming a point of concern to many. Issues of access, social equity, sustainability, technology design, technology dissemination and other related areas are constantly being addressed in conferences and development forums. The ICTD conferences, held annually since 2006 provide an international platforms for researchers and practitioners to explore ICT based solutions and possibilities. These conferences

N. A. Alias, *ICT Development for Social and Rural Connectedness*,
SpringerBriefs in Electrical and Computer Engineering,
DOI: 10.1007/978-1-4614-6901-8_2, © The Author(s) 2013

also support networking and have spawned many collaborative projects among members of different sectors, industry and education. Academic programs at the doctoral, postgraduate and undergraduate level are now offered by universities such as University of Colorado, Royal Holloway University of London and University of Manchester. Online courses are readily available as well (More information on ICTD is available at http://ictlogy.net/).

Key players of ICTD include UNESCO, World Bank, ITU (International Communication Union) and several others based in the different countries such as IDRC (International Development Research Centre) in Canada and SIDA (Swedish International Development Cooperation Agency).

ICTD is also very much related to the United Nations Millenium Development Goals (MDG) that comprise aims to end poverty and hunger, gender equality, universal education, child health, maternal health, combat HIV, environmental sustainability and global partnership. Due to the limited ability to acquire ICT among the rural people, the range of ICTs relevant to the users varies from radio to internet ready computers at tele-centers. In many instances, the convergence of ICTs is exploited to support the effort to enhance human capacity and empowerment, reduce poverty, strengthen communication, promote local content and knowledge and to ensure equitable access. Much of the concepts linking ICTs and development (or ICT4D) have been explored by Weigel and Waldburger (2004) as illustrated in Fig. 2.1.

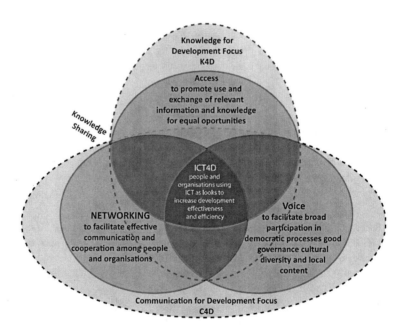

Fig. 2.1 Weigel and Walkdburger's framework for ICT4D: Key dimensions and main goals (*Source Weigel and Walkdburger* 2004)

The dimensions put forward in Weigel and Walkdburger's framework warrants an approach that is people centred and demand driven. It requires support and involvement from multiple stakeholders (government, NGOs, community) at the global, national and local level.

This brief zooms into the use of ICT in the microenvironment of people in local communities. However, it does not intend to discuss poverty reduction or demo-cratic processes; it centers on the perspective of the people and harps on the idea of ICT as a tool to connect.

2.1.1   ICT and the Rural Community Development

Digital divide, or more appropriately digital inclusion is one the main themes associated with ICTD. The gap between those who have ICT access and those who don't requires intervention to prevent it from widening. ICTD focuses on alleviating the destitute, marginalized and technology—disadvantaged groups of people. Rural communities are prime examples of these groups. Most govern-mental initiatives aim to bridge the digital divide between the urban and rural communities by increasing access to technology. In Malaysia, for instance, forty two RICs in the different states in Malaysia were established to dissemi-nate information via digital means and engage rural area citizens in its plans and transformation initiatives.

In the case of employing ICT for rural community development several points of concern need to be considered:

- Access: ICT needs to be equally accessible by the community members to allow acquisition of skills and knowledge sharing.
- Culture: local culture plays a role in the acceptance of ICT as a tool for personal capacity development and knowledge sharing.
- Utility and personal objectives: having access to ICT may not necessarily means maximizing the potential and capability of ICTs to improve one's wellbeing and personal growth.
- Beyond connectivity: the effective use of ICTs is not just a matter of having efficient infrastructure and speed of connections. It is also a question of how the people and community utilize ICT to connect.
- Relevant and people-centred applications: the impact of ICT use for rural development depends much on how relevant the technology is to the individual and the community he is in. Embedding ICTs in a rural community thus requires a thorough needs analysis.
- Theory of change and technology sustainability: change does not happen in a pre-defined fashion or strictly in accordance to some governmental plan. How a rural community evolves upon implementation of technology depends heavily on perceived needs of the community members and whether technology can be sustained and managed by the community.

The above points mirror most of Weigel *and Walkdburger* (2004)'s *framework*; making use of ICT for rural development therefore is not a straight-forward, easy task.

There are numerous rural ICT development projects in developing nations around the world. Early projects by UNESCO such as the Kothmale project depicted successful convergence of the internet and local community radio (Pringle and David 2002). Achievement of the project was on awareness and local capacity. Members of the rural community became aware, and used ICT I their daily lives. The Malaysian eBario is a pilot research project involving the innovative application of ICTs (Information and Communication Technologies) with the goal of continually sustaining social and economic programs in a rural community in Sarawak which does not have the basic amenities such as electricity, water and telecommunications. One of the innovation and key lessons learnt is that there is a need to focus on people and not just on technology. The project employed a participatory approach whereby the community members were involved in all phases of the project, from planning, implementation, to operation and maintenance of the project. A similar experience was reported by Fourie (2008) on the South Africa's program on the use of ICT to alleviate poverty and rural human development problems. The country policies and projects were found to assist the rural poor in improving their livelihoods. ICT was found to be most useful in practical matters such as communicating during a crisis, keeping in contact with family members and in assisting business. The sustainability of such projects however, requires local community involvement and necessary appropriation of ICT.

The OECD (development working paper by Caspary and O'Connor (2003)) gives a detailed and exhaustive account of various ICT access models and projects in Bangladesh, India, Mozambique, Salvador, Chile, Brazil and many others. They relate the necessity of initial subsidy, conducive regulatory environment, willingness to pay among rural people, local content, complementary infrastructure and services and NGOs as catalysts to ensure ICT serves the rural communities well. Galperin (2005)'s report on wireless networks in rural Latin America echoes some of Casper and O'Connor's concern on government subsidy, regulatory environment and a balance of cost and social and economic returns. While there appears to be potential in WLAN technologies to enhance connectivity in the rural areas, Galperin cautions a large-scale implementation due to to the lack of evidence in its long-term sustainability. Rao (2009) further discusses several aspects of ICT provision in rural India through projects aimed at enhancing access to information and communication, education, literacy development, entrepreneurship, health, governance and democracy. It was found that some projects fared well while others were less successful. Rao (2009) stated eight thrusts needed to meet the socio-economic aspirations of rural communities. These are connectivity provision, content creation, capacity augmentation, core technologies' creation and exploitation, cost reduction, competence building, community participation and community commitment. A local and particularistic approach is needed to empower rural people and reduce the digital divide.

There are countless government and non government ICT projects for rural community development; most of which are directed to provide connectivity that would inadvertently contribute to building local capacity.

The government of Malaysia spends billions on ICT infrastructure for both urban and rural areas. In 2001 under the Eighth Malaysia Plan (RMK 8) the Malaysian government had approved RM12 million (approx. USD 3.2 million) for the Information Technology division of the Ministry of Rural and Regional Development to implement the *Medan Infodesa* (*MID*) *Program, or* Rural Information Centre, a one stop ICT Centre for rural communities. Another RM9.5 million was also allocated for the ICT training (Final Outcome Report on ICT 2008). The main objective of the programs was to develop an integrated planning approach to create ICT awareness among rural population and to bridge the digital divide between rural and urban communities. The project started with 6 pilot projects in 2001 and by 2005 (at the end of the 8th Malaysia plan) 23 projects were operational and 19 in various stages of implementation (Final Outcome Report on ICT 2008).

The analysis of the outcome of the program for three villages in the state of Malacca was reported by the Malaysian Ministry of Rural and Regional Development in 2008 (Final report on the Rural ICT outcome 2008). It was found that 95 % of the participants who attended the training became more ICT savvy. Out of 109 respondents (30 % of the total number trained) 4 were categorized as not *ICT literate*, 57 as *ICT literate* and 48 as expert in ICT. The average number of users at the centers was around 173–547 per month depending on the village. It was reported that after the project, 69.72 % of the village residents owned computers.

Other ICT projects implemented under the Ministry of Rural and Regional Development include courses on using ICT to manage the rural areas. The objective of this project was to provide ICT awareness to the rural area heads, women and youth. At the same time it also aimed at increasing the use of ICT in their day-to-day affairs. From the project, 17 series of courses were implemented involving about 632 participants. Analysis of the results showed that there was a marked increase in the participants' knowledge of ICT. Thirty two (32 %) said they did not know anything about the components of a computer before the program while upon completing the program 95.5 % said they were more knowledgeable. With regard to the use of ICT in their daily lives; 40.9 % use them for official duties and 13.6 % use for personal use. For the personal use, 32 % is for surfing, 9 % data compilation, 9 % editing pictures, 9 % games, and 4.5 % chatting. The frequency of use: 23 % use daily, 18 % twice a week, 14 % once a week, and 14 % once a month.

Another initiative introduced by the government was the SchoolNet Project, a joint effort between the government and a few private sectors. The main objective of the project was to provide broadband infrastructure and Internet access to specific school sites (SchoolNet 2009). The SchoolNet Project was monitored by the Ministry of Education and Ministry of Energy, Water and Telecommunications. The target group were all schools throughout the country. Out of 9,406 schools, 75 % were in rural areas. However more research is needed to gauge the effectiveness of the program and to what extent the teachers and the schoolchildren have used the Internet and for what purpose. The GSB *TechnoGogy Learning in Schools* (GTL schools) project (2008–2009), a spin-off of the Schoolnet Project is yet another initiative that requires evaluation of its impact. Other projects include the

Gerakan Desa Wawasan (Vision Village Movement), *Titian Digital* (or the Digital Bridge) project and the eBario project for indigeneous people.

The focus of this brief is the *Pusat Internet Desa* or Rural Internet Centre (RIC) project that represents yet another move by the Malaysian government and nongovernmental organisation to provide ready access to ICT. As of 2010, forty two Rural Internet Centres (RICs) each with its own website and network of members are now available in Malaysia. The telecentre project initiated in April 2000 stands as one of the largest government's initiatives to bridge the rural–urban digital divide through free community-shared ICT facilities and internet access. The modest facility is hosted by the local postal office and managed by two personnel. The Malaysian government aims to set up such centres that will eventually reach an estimated 2.8 million members of the rural communities (Nor Iadah et al. 2008). The move is noble and appropriate. Rural communities need to stay abreast not only of technological advances but of the country's development and the government plans. A study was done by Hazita (2008) to look at the level of preparedness, the suitability as well as the ICT needs of the people in the rural areas that were considered as the critical groups namely, youth, women and the senior citizens. The research was based on an earlier report to UNESCO that found a clear gap between the urban areas and the rural areas with specific reference to youth in the use of ICT. It is important to note at this point that there are other public access ICT alternatives in Malaysia. These include public libraries, cyber cafés, Medan Infodesa (Village info-centres) and the Community Broadband Centres recently launched by the Malaysian government under different programs and ministries. The RICs however, are expected to reap their gains and benefits since they been in existence for almost 12 years.

2.1.2 ICT and Personal Capacity Development

Personal capacity development deals with increasing knowledge and skills of people within the context of their lives. This includes enhancing their capability to improve their working and living conditions. The use of ICT for inclusion and personal capacity development of those with disabilities have been widely spread. In terms of capacity development of rural people, projects are more often targeted at community capacity building than at the personal or individual level. Then again, empowering rural people especially women has been the agenda of many NGOs and government initiatives (Macueve et al. 2009). Within the limitations of this brief, rural people personal capacity development via ICT will be reported based on what they perceived as empowering them to conduct their day-to-day tasks.

Most ICTD project reports center on connectivity and issues of community development on a macro level perspective. This brief turns to a micro level context of connectedness of the rural people. A brief overview of ICT and connectedness is essential before rural connectedness is presented.

2.2 ICT and Connectedness

Of late, researchers have argued about the capability of technology to provide a sense of connectedness that encompasses a sense of belonging, sharing and a feeling of being touch (Haans and IJsselsteijn 2006; Rettie 2003; Yukawa et al. 2008). As mentioned earlier, synchronous and asynchronous communication media may lead to a strong feeling of connectedness and may contribute to feelings of relatedness and closeness, as they provide opportunity for interaction over geographical distance (Van Bel et al. 2010). This is also illustrated by Castro (2007) who studied community connectedness and the use of information and communication technology to increase the sense of connection between migrants and their community of origin. He argues that the migrants require certain information elements and tools to heighten such connectedness.

Research has also shown that ICT influences various dimensions of social connectedness. The CareRabbit e-health research conducted to enable family to stay in touch with a hospitalized child (Blom et al. 2011) demonstrates the enhancement of wellbeing and social connectedness via ICT. The Waag Society publishes research findings that promulgate ICT as a means to increase social interaction with elderly (Waag Society 2012). The Human Technology Interaction Group is an example of active group of researchers working on ICT on social connectedness. Van Bel et al. (2009) ascertained four dimensions of social connectedness, three of which were found to be heightened computer mediated shared subjective experiences termed as I-Sharing. The three dimensions were shared understandings, knowing each others' experiences, and feelings of closeness. Van Gennip (2012) explored the effects of mediated heartbeat communication on social connectedness at the personal level. Despite the absence of any significant effect, the research suggests future possibilities of ICT and social connectedness research. There is little doubt that social connectedness via ICT will soon be emerge as a field of its own.

On a more general note, ICT has also spurred educational engagement among students and the well being of the elderly and young children. ICT connectedness tends to assist work related tasks of office workers as well (Leung 2011). Community connectedness through community portals such as The GraniteNet (www.granitenet.com.au) is also becoming more prevalent.

2.2.1 Social Network, Social Media and Government Connectedness

Social networks can be accessed across geographical boundaries between people who may never have met. A study by Koebler et al. (2010) suggests that the use of status update messaging generates a feeling of connectedness between users. The feeling of being connected is reported to be in relation to the amount of messages and not the type of information an individual is sharing among his or her network.

Social media has undoubtedly been extensively used to connect. In October 2012 Facebook announced that there are now one billion people using Facebook every month. Leaders of institutions are using Facebook to connect. The vice chancellor of a Malaysian university boasts a number of more than 100,000 friends among students and academic staff. The platform to connect is now at a click.

Studies on ICT applications in the government include those applications that provide decision support to administrators, improve services to citizens and empower citizens to access information and knowledge (Bhatnagar 2000). In terms of government connectedness, Curtin (2006) in his report on E–Government list five stages of E-Government namely:

- *Emerging Presence.* Stage I e-government presents information which is limited and basic comprising of web page and/or an official website.
- *Enhanced Presence.* In Stage II the government provides greater public policy and governance sources of current and archived information.
- *Interactive Presence.* By Stage III the online services of the government enter the interactive mode with services to enhance convenience of the consumer.
- *Transactional Presence.* Stage IV allows two-way interactions between the citizen and his/her government.
- *Networked Presence.* Stage V represents the most sophisticated level in online egovernment initiatives. It can be characterized by the integration of G2G [government-to-government], G2C [government-to-citizen], and C2G [citizen-togovernment] (and reverse) interactions.

(Adapted from Curtin 2006)

The government needs to connect and to feel the pulse of its people, both urban and rural communities. Hence there must be a move from the transactional presence or stage IV of e-government to the network presence stage. And for this, many governments especially in the developed countries have launched their government 2.0 initiatives to be in line with the evolution of the web from web 1.0 to web 2.0 and of late, web 3.0. Government 2.0 initiatives include (1) mash-up services such as GIS, weather, traffic and tax services (2) Citizen-oriented services and improved accessibility through portals, mobile devices, TV etc. and (3) use of 'blogs' and 'wikis' to strengthen and expand participation by citizens and government workers (The Canadian National Information Society Agency 2008). Australian Centrelink and Britain's Connecting Britain are two examples of successful government initiatives. In Malaysia, the federal government launched the Malaysia.gov.my portal to offer services of both interactive and informative nature. The Government *Pemudah* website is another service to facilitate public services delivery where the citizens may provide feedback to a special task force of 23 highly respected individuals from both the public and private sectors via emails and feedback form available on the website. Other recent initiatives include the Prime Minister's blog and facebook.

Access to the internet thus provides higher level of connectedness as people are able to access information resulting in opportunities to participate and interact in their social network and society.

The discussion thus far, suggests that ICT supports many facets of connectedness. It is not merely a tool or a platform to connect. The disparity may rests in the access and form of ICT available to the person or the community. The more affluent societies typically enjoy the latest ICT tools and gadgets in the privacy of their own home or within their personal space. Others in the remote areas are by and large less prosperous and hence depend on government supported facility and/or NGO initiatives. The next section considers ICT and rural connectedness. Due to the differences between rural and urban ICT access and willingness to pay for services, rural connectedness will be viewed from a developmental perspective.

2.3 ICT and Rural Connectedness

The study of rural connectedness is a facet of ICT and rural community development research. Authors such as Reading (2010), Rao (2009) and Fourie (2008) described projects and research conducted on leveraging ICT to connect to communities in large and sparse countries such as Australia, India and Africa. Reading (2010) for instance, addresses the geographical isolation of Australian teachers and suggested the delivery of professional development modules via synchronous and asynchronous technology. The use of ICT to increase the professional connectedness of these teachers enhances reciprocal interaction, development of communities of practice, awareness of pedagogy and collegial and critical practices. The Worldbank has intensively embarked on similar projects; ICT in agriculture is an initiative the worldbank has taken to connect rural small holders to knowledge, networks and institutions (The World Bank Group 2012).

Rural connectedness has in fact evolved as reported by Alias et al. (2010) and Craig and Greenhill (2005). Craig and Greenhill (2005) for instance see the shift towards greater levels of connectedness in terms of

- Rural areas are increasingly using broadband to create supportive local relationships and to build social cohesion;
- Rural areas are accessing new resources and opportunities through broadband, changing the relationship between centres and peripheries;
- People and resources are moving out from urban centres towards the most connected rural areas.

(Craig and Greenhill 2005)

In terms of applications, more rural youths are on using social media to communicate. More often than not, rural connectedness entails the existence of a tele-centre or community centres. In particular, a study by London et al. (2006) indicates two types of ties that are fostered through community technology centers. These are (1) bonding ties within communities that are horizontal (peer to peer) and (2) bridging ties to individuals who are not aligned in social status or geographic location. The first tie thus enhances supportive relationships and opportunities to belong while the

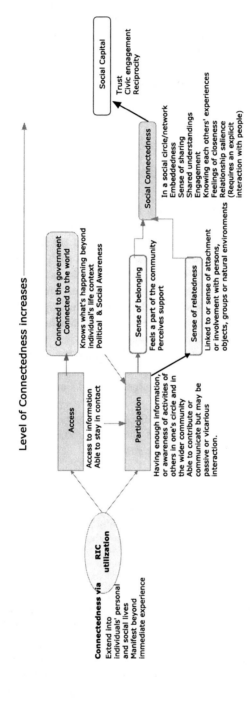

Fig. 2.2 A framework of connectedness among Malaysian RIC users (Adapted from Alias et al. forthcoming, 2013)

second tie provides the chance to connect to a world different from one's own. A report on the strength of internet ties by Boase et al. (2006) describes,

> The connectedness that the internet and other media foster within social networks has real payoffs: People use the internet to seek out others in their networks of contacts when they need help (pp. 2).

In the context of this chapter, both ties will be explored in the light of a typology of connectedness to be presented in the next section.

Akin to Markham et al. (2010) and Libbey (2004), several constructs are considered when studying connectedness among rural community members. Generally, ICT access is via public access sites such as tele-centers and internet centers. In relation these common sites, it is postulated that connectedness begins with initial access as shown in Fig. 2.1. In this framework, it is inferred that with access to information and to other people, rural people are able to stay connected. This leads to participation; a sense of relatedness and sense of belonging emerge out of it. Connectedness is therefore evolves on a continuum.

Figure 2.2 illustrates the various constructs that frame the connectedness of rural Malaysians. These constructs are based on literature and the initial findings of a research on ICT and rural connectedness, to be discussed in the next chapter. Due to limited capability to acquire ICT on an individual basis, having access and participation are seen as precedents to higher levels of connectedness. The Rural Internet Centre (RIC) thus plays a crucial role in providing this access to the rural poor.

In short, this brief studies how public access sites, in this case the Malaysian Rural Internet Centres impact the connectedness of its users with friends, family, nation and state leaders through the utilization of various ICT tools and Government 2.0 initiatives.

References

Alias NA, Jamaludin H, Hashim S, Ismail IS, Suhaili N (2010) Theories of change and evaluation of Malaysian rural internet centers. Paper presented at the ICTD 2010 conference, London, 13–16 Dec 2010

Alias NA, Mohd Noor M, Proenza JP, Jamaludin H, Ismail IS, Hashim S, Sulaiman (forthcoming, 2013) Impact of public access to computers and the internet on the connectedness of rural Malaysians in ICT and social change: the impact of public access to computers and the Internet, Amy Mahan research fellowship program

Bhatnagar S (2000) Social implications of ICT in developing countries: lessons from Asian success stories. Electron J Inf Syst Develop Ctry 1(4):1–9

Blom SR, Boere-Boonekamp MM, Stegwee RA (2011) Social connectedness through ICT and the influence on wellbeing: the case of the CareRabbit. Stud Health Technol Inform 2011(169):78–82

Boase J, Horrigan JB, Wellman B, Rainie L (2006) The strength of internet ties. Pew Internet and American Life Project, Washington, DC

Caspary G, O'Connor D (2003) Providing low cost information technology access to rural communities in developing countries: What works? What pays? Working Paper No. 229, OECD Development Centre, Paris

Castro LA (2007) Connectedness: support to communities in diaspora via ICT. In: Proceedings of the conference on human factors in computing systems, pp 1629–1632

Craig J, Greenhill B (2005) Beyond Digital Divides? The future of ICT in ruralareas. Commission for Rural Communities, Cheltenham

Centers for Disease Control and Prevention (2009). School connectedness: Strategies forincreasing protective factors among youth. Atlanta, GA: U.S. Department of Health and Human Services

Curtin GG (2006) Issues and challenges global e-government/e-participation models, measurement and methodology: a framework for moving forward. Workshop on e-participation and e-government: understanding the present and creating the future, Budapest, Hungary, 27–28 July 2006

Final Outcome Report on ICT (2008) Ministry of Rural and Regional Development, Malaysia

Fourie L (2008) Enhancing the livelihoods of the rural poor through ICT: a knowledge map. InfoDev working paper 13, South Africa country study

Galperin H (2005) Wireless networks and rural development: opportunities for Latin America, The Massachusetts Institute of Technology, Information Technologies and International Development, vol 2, 3rd edn. Spring 2005, pp 47–56

Haans A, Ijsselsteijn W (2006) Mediated social touch: a review of current research and future directions. Virtual Real 9(2–3):149–159

Hazita A (2008) Rural social transformation for the 21st century:impact of e-community centers on the development of e-literacy among youth in rural areas in Malaysia. Jurnal Pembangunan Belia Malaysia 1 (Disember) 2008, 83–98

Kobler F, Riedl C, Vetter C, Leimeister JM, Krcmar H (2010) Social connectedness on facebook—an explorative study on status message usage. In: Proceedings of the sixteenth Americas conference on information systems, Lima, Peru

Leung L (2011) Effects of ICT connectedness, permeability, flexibility, and negative spillovers on burnout and job and family satisfaction. Human Technol 7(3):250–267

Libbey HP (2004) Measuring student relationships to school: attachment, bonding, connectedness, and engagement. J Sch Health 74(7):274–283

London RA, Pastor M, Servon LS, Rosner R, Wallace A (2006) The role of community technology centers in youth skill-building and empowerment. Center for justice, tolerance and community working paper, University of California, Santa Cruz

Macueve G, Mandlate J, Ginger L, Gaster P, Macome E (2009) Women's use of information and communication technologies in Mozambique: a tool for empowerment? In: Buskens I, Webb A (eds) African women & ICTs: investigating technology, gender and empowerment (pp 21–32). Zed Books, London and New York

Markham CM, Lormand D, Gloppen KM, Peskin MF, Flores B, Low B, House L (2010) Connectedness as a predictor of sexual and reproductive health. J Adolesc Health 46:23–42

Nor Iadah Y, Huda I, Razak RA, Osman WRS (2008) Assessment of rural internet centres (RICs) web pages. In: Proceedings of the 1st regional conference on human resource development (RESERD 2008), Primula Beach Resort, Kuala Terengganu, Terengganu, Malaysia, 14–15 Jan, pp 50–58

Pringle I, David MJR (2002) Rural community ICT applications: the Kothmale model. Electron J Inf Syst Develop Ctry 8:1–14

Rao S (2009) Role of ICTs in Indian rural communities. 5 July 2009. http://www.ci-journal.net/index.php/ciej/article/view/313/429. Accessed 25 Dec 2012

Reading C (2010) Using ICT to increase professional connectedness for teachers in remote Australia. Aust Educ Comput 25(2):3–6

Rettie R (2003) Connectedness, awareness and social presence. 6th International Presence Workshop, Aalborg. http://www.kingston.ac.uk/~ku03468/includes/docs/Connectedness,%20Awareness%20and%20Social%20Presence.pdf. Accessed 13 Nov 2012

The Canadian National Information Society Agency (2008) Concepts and features of government 2.0 and 3.0. Retrieved 9 Nov 2009 from: www.mikekujawski.ca/ftp/Government2.0and3.0.pdf

The Social Report (2010) New Zealand Ministry of Social Development. www.socialreport.msd.govt.nz/social-connectedness. Accessed 15 June 2010

The World Bank Group (2012) ICT for greater development impact. http://siteresources. worldbank.org/EXTINFORMATIONANDCOMMUNICATIONANDTECHNOLOGIES/ Resources/WBG_ICT_Strategy-2012.pdf. Accessed 15 Nov 2012

Van Bel D, Smolders K, IJsselsteijn W, De Kort Y (2009) Social connectedness: concept and measurement. In: Callaghan V, Kameas A, Reyes A, Royo D, Weber M (eds) Proceedings of the 5th international conference on international conferences on intelligence environments. IOS Press, Armsterdam, pp 67–74

Van Bel D, Smolders K, IJsselsteijn W, De Kort Y (2010) How intimate mediated interaction affects social connectedness. Etmaal van de Communicatiewetenschap. http://togather.eu/ handle/123456789/430. Accessed 14 June 2012

Van Gennip, DAP (2012) Social pulse: the effects of mediated heartbeat communication on social connectedness, liking and pro-social behavior, Unpublished master of science thesis, Eindhoven University

Waag Society (2012) Real needs for real people. http://waag.org/sites/waag/files/ public/Publicaties/CLL_brochure_lowres.pdf. Accessed 20 Nov 2012

Weigel G, Waldburger D (eds) (2004) ICT4D—connecting people for a better world: lessons, innovations and perspectives of information and communication technologies for development. SDC and GKP, Berne. www.globalknowledge.org/ict4d

Yukawa T, Kawano K, Suzuki Y, Suriyon T, Fukumura Y (2008) Implementing a sense of connectedness in e-learning. In: Luca J, Weippl E (eds) Proceedings of world conference on educational multimedia, hypermedia and telecommunications 2008. AACE, Chesapeake, VA, pp 1198–1207. http://www.editlib.org/p/28538. Accessed 27 Oct 2009

Chapter 3
A Case of Rural Connectedness: The Malaysian Rural Internet Center (RICs) Users' Experience

3.1 An Overview of the Malaysian RICs

The rural internet centres in Malaysia were established in two phases in the year 2000 and 2003. The project started in April 2000 by the Ministry of Energy, Water, and Communication of Malaysia stands as one of the government's initiatives to bridge the rural–urban digital divide through free community-shared ICT facilities and internet access. The objectives include giving rural folks the exposure, awareness, enhancement of skills and ultimately building their capacities. The Malaysian government aimed to set up 240 such centres by the year 2010 which would eventually reach an estimated 2.8 million members of the rural communities.

The main objective of the establishment of the RICs is to bridge the digital divide between the urban and rural communities by increasing access to technology. With the forty-two RICs in the different states in Malaysia (Refer Table 3.1), the government is set to disseminate information via digital means and engage rural area citizens in its plans and transformation initiatives. Government 2.0 tools and services such as the 1 Malaysia portal and the prime minister's blog are now fully operational and accessible to those living in urban areas. What would be a better platform than the RICs to provide the same access to the rural communities.

The rural internet centres are hosted in the community post office building and are open weekdays from 8 a.m. to 5 p.m. Each of the RIC (visited) has separate entrance from the post office thus avoiding non intending users to utilize the RIC facility. The RICS have the basic facility to support their operation (electricity, internet connection, etc.). Cable broadband connection is available at each RIC. The number of computers varies from one RIC to another. Basically the area allotted to each RIC limits the number of computers in the centre. The biggest number of computers reported in the RICs was eight computers. The centres enjoy support from village committees and officers from the Ministry who monitor each centre's activities. Basically, the RICs are supposed to be manned by two personnel—the manager and the assistant manager. These are amicable and friendly personnel; they have very positive relationship with the users. The manager and/or assistant manager is seen

N. A. Alias, *ICT Development for Social and Rural Connectedness*,
SpringerBriefs in Electrical and Computer Engineering,
DOI: 10.1007/978-1-4614-6901-8_3, © The Author(s) 2013

Table 3.1 Rural internet centres (RIC) in Malaysia

State	Number of RICs	Rural internet centre sites
Sabah	3	Tenom, Kota Belud, Kota Marudu
Sarawak	4	Mukah, Betong, Bau, Song
Perlis	1	Simpang Empat
Kedah	4	Bukit Kayu Hitam, Yan, Kuala Nerang, Kupang
Pulau Pinang	2	Tasek Glugor, Balik Pulau
Perak	5	Selama, Kuala Kurau, Langkap, Tanjung Malim, Parit
Selangor	6	Beranang, Sungai Pelek, Rasa, Hulu Langat, Tanjung Sepat, Sungai Air Tawar
Negri Sembilan	3	Kota, Lenggeng, Bandar Seri Jempol
Melaka	1	Tanjung Kling
Johor	6	Bandar Tenggara, Bandar Penawar, Labis, Pagoh, Sungai Mati, Sri Medan
Pahang	3	Sungai Koyan, Bukit Goh, Bandar Tun Razak
Trengganu	2	Besut, Marang
Kelantan	2	Kuala Krai, Kuala Balah
	42	

Source http://www.pid.net.my/

by the users as pertinent and almost indispensable. They were respected, regarded as "knowledgeable and friendly" and typically referred to as "cikgu (teacher)" by the rural users. The users confirmed their need of the RIC staff as they "have helped the local community, open our eyes to ICT and assist us in gaining more knowledge".

3.1.1 Services at the RICs

The basic service offered by the RICs is the use of ICT tools at regular opening hours. Users may come into search the internet or use the computers and other peripherals to prepare documents. Most RICs charge a small amount of RM 1–RM 2 (€0.20–€0.45) per hour of use. All the RICs conduct scheduled training sessions in basic computer, internet and Microsoft applications such as MS Word, MS Excel and MS Powerpoint. The training is packaged at only RM 20–RM 50(€5–€12) per package depending on the RIC. One of the RIC does not charge for the training they give to senior citizens.

3.1.2 General RIC User Profile

RIC users are school going adolescents, youths, housewives, entrepreneurs and senior citizens. More female users (45–80 % of the users) are reported to frequent the centres. Senior citizens who frequented the RICs were normally men. The younger users do not have internet connected computers in their homes while the older users normally have PCs or laptops in their homes. They however, visit the centres for

ICT support and training. Almost 50 % of the RICs surveyed reported disabled user. Mentally challenged users are also frequenting some of the RICs.

It is not the intention of this brief to dispel every aspects of RIC utilization among rural Malaysians. The main idea is to illustrate how the use of ICT via the Rural Internet Centres (RICs) impacts the users' connectedness and capacity development. It is also the purpose of the brief to explore government connectedness among the RIC users. Even though only forty-two RICs were actually established in the two phases, their achievements have been reported and published despite the reports been few and isolated. The RICs are believed to provide rural communities with similar ICT services and with such provision, rural folks would have access to information, increase their ICT skills, able to conduct various transactions and to communicate with friends, families and also the government. The most common theory of change logic model associated with the RICs is explicated in Fig. 3.1.

The RIC was observed to be developing into a community infrastructure that would be utilized when the users felt a need to do so. Users come in for one or more purposes

1. To be trained
2. To use the facility on their own
3. To seek help from RIC staff.

Other than scheduled training, the three main purposes for frequenting the centres were

4. Using the computers for typing and preparing documents for school, work and business
5. Finding information on the internet
6. Communicating with friends and acquaintances.

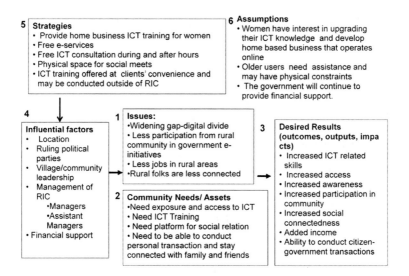

Fig. 3.1 Theory of change logic model for most Malaysian RICs (Alias et al. 2010)

3.2 Measuring Connectedness and Personal Capacity Development Through ICT Utilization at the RIC

3.2.1 Measures of Connectedness

The main instrument used to measure connectedness and empowerment was on online survey that consisted of items generated in relation to the constructs mentioned in Chap. 1. 17-items were generated to gauge connectedness. The respondents were asked whether they have used the RIC to for communication with family and friends in the last 12 months. They were also required to provide reasons for not utilizing the RIC. Further probe was conducted on whether

their communication level with their family had increased
their communication level with their friends had increased
they consistently used social networking sites to keep in touch with friends and family members
they felt their social network had widened.

Further questions were asked regarding access, participation, involvement, sense of relatedness and sense of belonging

Access and Participation

Have you joined or are you joining any activities, classes or attending courses held in the community (e.g., computer classes, debate, drama, band) at the RIC this year?
By accessing the internet at the RIC, to what extent are you aware of the activities carried out by family members who live far away?
By accessing the internet at the RIC, to what extent are you aware of the activities carried out by friends who live far away?
To what extent are you informed of the activities of NGOs or charity groups via the use of internet at the RIC?
To what extent do you contribute ideas by commenting/writing in others' blogs?
To what extent do you contribute (e.g. leave comments, sending messages, chat) in online social network?

Involvement, Sense of relatedness and Sense of belonging

To what extent is your involvement in any online club, society, or other online community?
To what extent do you feel connected to your community leader via non formal access at the RIC?
To what extent do you feel connected when you are aware of the plans and activities carried out by family members and friend who live far away?
To what extent do you think feel you can contribute and share with others in your social network?
To what extent do you feel you are part of the social network of which you are a member?

3.2.2 Measure of Government Connectedness

Government connectedness is measured by eliciting RIC user's detail in relation to three categories of government tools and services.

Access or use of education and job-related government web services
Use of online government transactions i.e. to pay bills, taxes, insurance etc.
Use of government 2.0 tools such as the Prime Minister's Facebook account, Twitter etc.

3.2.3 Measure of Personal Capacity Development

Personal capacity development was measured according to three constructs

Increased personal ICT-related skills
Access to information and tools
Ability to conduct transactions (personal and citizen-government transactions).

Thirteen questions were asked based on the constructs and respondent were requested to note their agreement based on a 5 point Likert scale. The questions are as follows.

Increased personal ICT related skills: Compared to before having access to internet via RIC

I can now use the computer to type letters and stuff
I can now search for information on employment opportunities
I can now apply for jobs/apply for university placement
I can now use emails to communicate with my family and friends

Access to information: Compared to before having access to internet via RIC

It is now relatively easy to get information about what is happening in my community
It is now relatively easy to get information about what is happening in my country
It is now relatively easy to get information about what is happening to my family and friends
It is now relatively easy to get information about entertainment
It is now relatively easy to get information about the price and availability of products I consume
It is now relatively easy to get information about my education/children's education

Ability to conduct online transactions: Compared to before having access to internet via RIC

It is now relatively easy to advertise my products and run my business
It is now relatively easy to conduct government related transactions (pay tax etc.) without leaving my village
It is now relatively easy to pay bills

3.3 Impact of ICT Access on Personal Capacity Development

An overview of the general impact of public access to ICT is provided before proceeding to specific impact on connectedness and empowerment. The findings were derived from both quantitative and qualitative responses of 299 RIC users in the online survey. As explained earlier, the users were asked to rate the impact of ICT access on various aspects of their lives based on a five point scale ranging from 2 (highly positive) to −2 (highly negative). No impact was registered as zero. Impact of ICT through RIC utilization was perceived at two levels or tiers:

- Direct impact on ICT related skills
- Indirect impact on aspects that emerge from the acquisition of ICT related skills.

Most users reported the first tier impact. On a higher level, access to ICT via RIC utilization has been perceived as impacting various aspects of the users lives including their knowledge, skills, social networks, and business. The 13–17 year old users recounted their communication with friends as being most impacted while the other age groups rated the highest impact on their knowledge and education. Thematic analysis of user responses produced several other categories of impact perceived by the users that included

- self confidence
- wider social network
- life enhancement
- future needs.

The users also perceived higher order impacts such as acculturation of ICT in one's life, task efficiency and business proliferation via ICT usage at the RIC (See Table 3.2).

Table 3.2 Perceived impact

Aspect	Female rating (maximum rating = 2)	Male rating (maximum rating = 2)	Rating average (maximum rating = 2)
Knowledge and education	1.68	1.60	1.65
Access to resources and needed skills required for jobs and personal tasks	1.65	1.52	1.60
Communication with family members and friends	1.58	1.59	1.59
Access to government information and services	1.42	1.40	1.41
Hobby, interest and social work	1.40	1.35	1.38
Meeting new people (face to face or online)	1.39	1.34	1.37
Leisure	1.41	1.32	1.37
Health	1.22	1.21	1.22
Business and Income	1.22	1.12	1.18
Receive or transfer fund to family/friends	1.16	1.08	1.13

Table 3.3 Mean rating of perceived impact according to age groups

Aspect (maximum rating = 2)	13–17	18–24	25–35	36–50	Above 50
Knowledge and education	1.33	**1.76**	**1.70**	**1.82**	**1.40**
Access to resources and needed skills required for jobs and personal tasks	1.54	1.64	1.66	1.58	1.50
Communication with family members and friends	**1.58**	1.65	1.59	1.58	1.10
Access to government information and services	1.14	1.45	1.49	1.56	1.00
Hobby, interest and social work	1.11	1.46	1.44	1.64	0.83
Meeting new people (face to face or online)	1.17	1.41	1.56	1.22	1.00
Leisure	1.3	1.43	1.43	1.5	1.00
Health	0.79	1.28	1.44	1.25	1.08
Business and Income	0.86	1.09	1.25	1.50	1.15
Receive or transfer fund to family/friends	0.3	1.22	1.30	1.04	0.67

The users rated lowest on ICT impact on their health and money sent/received. They responded positively on impact of ICT access on their knowledge and education.

In terms of gender, the impact was perceived in a similar manner by both genders except for the perceived impact of ICT on access to resources and needed skills which was found to be significantly different at a significant level of 0.1 ($p = 0.057$, $\alpha = 0.1$). The male users only exceeded the female users in their perceived impact on communication with family members. The difference, nonetheless is not significant.

The impact perceived by the different age groups is tabulated below in Table 3.3. The highest impact according to the age groups is highlighted in bold. Again, most users rated their knowledge and education as most impacted by the access to ICT. Interestingly secondary school- goers did not rate this aspect highly.

This was again echoed in the qualitative responses they provided in the survey. A thematic analysis produced several categories of impact perceived by the users that included

1. computer and internet skills
2. knowledge
3. self confidence
4. communication
5. wider social network
6. life enhancement
7. income and business
8. future needs.

The perceived impact can be further grouped into (1) direct or first level impact that constitute ICT awareness and acquisition of ICT skills and (2) a second level impact that stemmed out from the awareness and acquisition of skills. Most users recounted the direct impact of ICT. Users gave an account of being "IT blind to IT savvy" and "now able to type documents for my office". A user narrated

> I come from the village with no idea of what or how to use a computer. A friend introduced me to the center and I signed up for the computer course, I am still attending the training, my knowledge of computers have increased..I am so thankful to RIC.

Another wrote

> From an IT blind person, I am now proud to have learned ICT. Many did not think I would be able to use the computer because I am just a full time housewife. Now I am still attending the class at the RIC. I have also subscribed to the internet, got a notebook with the help of the RIC personnel and now, almost everyone in the family is ICT literate.

while a lady stated

> There are still many housewives and women who are shy and lack confidence to learn the computer and the internet. With RIC personnel who are friendly and able to spur the interest of this group, I am sure they (the group) will not be outdated and will be a housewife who is knowledgeable and can run an online business..

On another level, acculturation of ICT in their lives was mentioned by several users as an outcome of their exposure to ICT. Users gave accounts of how ICT access promoted their self confidence and regarded ICT knowledge and skills as "a valuable asset in my life". A number of users discovered ICT as a means for them to "be an informed and knowledgeable person", "enhance my social awareness" and to "stay abreast of the changing world". Others recognized the impact on various facets of their lives in. A young user wrote "I managed to complete and get high marks for my History paper with the help of the RIC manager". An entrepreneur "got to know other Entrepreneurial club members and able to market my products using email, facebook and blog as suggested by teacher Ija (reference to the RIC manager)". A senior citizen utilized the RIC to "prepare effective tutoring materials with MSWord and graphics". Users also saw the impact of ICT access on "improving (my) living standards" and their preparation to "further studies or get a job as the ICT skills that I acquired will enhance my achievement in the cyber world". Enhanced communication with family and friends were cited in 22 written responses. A user wrote "I make new friends and feel closer to those who are living far way". Another stated that he was "able to get in touch with my old friends".

A user claimed that it was "easier for us housewives to get culinary info and business" while another married the RIC manager. A user termed the RIC as a Multi-Information Centre that significantly impacted his access to information.

3.3.1 Selected Cases of Personal Capacity Development

Three cases of personal capacity development are presented below. The first two cases described older adult capacity development albeit with slightly different perspectives while the third case presented a women capacity for entrepreneur development.

> Uncle J. was a sixty seven year old retired government officer. He taught English on a part time basis to the community school children. He utilized the RIC to develop his lesson handouts and notes and to "keep up with what today's children are familiar to". He particularly felt empowered after taking up photography as a hobby at such "an old age" and described it as "something extra that I can do". Uncle J. felt "technically competent" due to his ability to capture and then worked on his digital images using the related software. He was very keen and motivated with his new hobby and was grateful to the RIC personnel who taught him the use of IT tools.

> Seventy two (72) year old Mr M. headed the village religious congregation. As an "imam" or Moslem priest, he led prayers and gave sermons to the community. Mr. M visited the RIC daily for assistance in preparing documents and to keep up with the latest information. He also utilized the RIC for social purposes such as meeting the community members. He regarded ICT as an important tool that alleviated his ability to perform his social duty and charity work. He rated his capability to access information especially those related to charity groups and NGOs highly. Mr. M described his ICT use at the RIC as easing his tasks, opening his mind and enhances his social work.

> Mrs. F was a single mother with five children. She started selling traditional cakes to fill her time but was driven to full time business when her husband passed away several years ago. She became an active member of the social entrepreneurs' club and was trained by the RIC staff to use email and blog to reach her customer. Her product marketing had gone online and her income had increased over the years.

Other cases of entrepreneurial capacity building were reported by other RICs. A case worth mentioning was the online shop or e-kedai developed by the Ministry to showcase the products of rural small businesses. Currently, 130 entrepreneurial initiatives are listed on the website http://www.pid.net.my/SCstores.cfm.

The findings described above showed that RIC users perceived (1) Increased personal ICT-related skills and (2) Access to information and services. There was evidence of one's ability to conduct online transaction but it was still minimal. The RIC has provided older adults and housewives a comfortable venue to learn and use ICT in their daily lives. Since most of them were at the initial stage of learning and utilizing ICT, their perceived impact was mostly at the personal level of capacity development.

3.4 Impact of ICT Access on Connectedness

In order to measure the perceived impact of access to ICT via RIC utilization on connectedness, users were asked on their use of RIC for communication purpose and to rate several aspects such as access, participation, involvement, sense of relatedness and sense of belonging.

Table 3.4 Access to information

	Strongly agree (%)	Agree (%)	Neutral (%)	Strongly agree (%)	Strongly disagree (%)
Easier access to information on events and happenings in my community	28.6	49.3	16.1	1.0	0.7
Easier access to information on events and happenings in my country	31.1	51.1	14.1	0.3	0.3
Easier access to information on what is happening to my family/friends living far away	23.7	50.3	19.4	1.3	1.0

3.4.1 Impact on Access and Participation

A high percentage of the users reported ease of access to information regarding family, friends, community and country as a result of ICT utilization at the RIC. Table 3.4 depicts the percentage response to the Likert scale items.

3.4.2 Participation in Online Informal Network

The users who utilize the RIC for communication purposes reported an increase in their level of communication with family members and friends. 87 % reported consistent communication via their social network. 86.1 % also reported an increase in their social network. All age groups experienced a wider social network except for the older adults. It is also interesting to note that there were users who did not experience such increase, 64 % of whom were younger users who tend to interact online with the same group they see in school or in the community they live in. They had not ventured much outside the community and were only beginning to build a larger network upon learning internet skills. In terms of gender, males and female users responded similarly to the above questions.

3.4.3 Awareness of Family Members' and Friends' Activities

Users are asked to rate their awareness level of activities of family members and friends living far away on a scale of 0 (none) to 6 (extremely). The levels are categorized as below:

0   No awareness
1–2   Low level of awareness
3–4   Moderate level of awareness
5–6   High level of awareness.

Overall, users rated their awareness at an average scale of 3.35 (friends), 3.21 (family members) and 2.41 (NGOs). This does not signify a high level of awareness among the users; it illustrates only a moderate level of awareness. However, 23.4 % of the users rated highly (5 or 6) in terms of awareness of family members' activities and another 22.8 % rated highly (5 or 6) in terms of awareness of friends' activities, most of whom were users below 25 years of age (57.4 %). Nevertheless, a 79 year old single woman recounted her use of email to stay in touch with her nephew who was working overseas. She also maintained a Facebook account to stay informed of friends' activities.

Figure 3.2 shows the level of awareness according to age groups. As expected, a relatively higher level of awareness is conveyed by users in the age groups of 18–35. Older adults are more informed of NGO activities compared to the other age groups with 21.1 % of the users having no information of NGO or charity group activities. Other than a few isolated cases, most RIC users did not utilize the ICT to enhance their social or civic awareness.

The RIC users were also asked on the extent they contribute ideas by commenting/writing in others' blogs and the extent they contribute (e.g. leave comments, sending messages, chat) in their online social network. The users rated their contribution to blogs at a rating average of 2.30 (0-none, 6-extremely); they contributed more in their online social network (rating average 3.38). 26.9 % of the users rated this contribution highly (5 or 6). Older adults and youths below 17 did not contribute highly to blogs; however a significant percentage of the youths tend to contribute highly to their social network. Figure 3.3 shows the percentage of high contribution to blogs or social networks according to age

A significant difference between male and female users is observed only in terms of non involvement. A significantly higher proportion of females was not informed of NGO activities and had not contributed ideas to others' blogs compared to the male users.

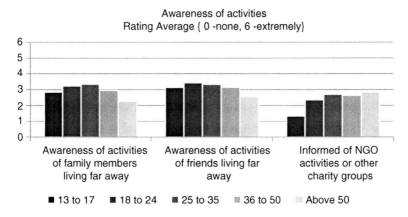

Fig. 3.2 Awareness of activities according to age groups

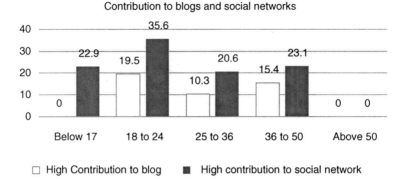

Fig. 3.3 Percentage of high contribution to blogs or social Networks (Rating of 5 or 6)

3.4.4 Involvement, Relatedness and Sense of Belonging

In measuring involvement, relatedness and sense of belonging, users were asked to rate (1) the extent of their involvement in online groups or communities, (2) the extent they feel they can contribute and share with others in their social network, (3) the extent they feel they are part of the social network of which they are a member, (4)the extent they feel connected when they are aware of the plans and activities carried out by family members and friends who live far away and (5) the extent they feel connected to their community leader via non formal access at the RIC.

Figure 3.4 depicts how the users rated their involvement in online groups or communities. These include interest groups and associations. Users rated a low level of involvement with a percentage of 21.1 % registering no such involvement at all. A comparison between male and female users was also made. Female users registered a slightly higher rating average of 2.37. However, statistical tests did not indicate any significant difference between the genders for moderate to high involvement. As a matter of fact, there was no significant difference between the genders for all the items tested which include

Feels connected to the community leader
Feels a part of the social network
Feels one can contribute and share in one's social network
Feels a part of the online social network
Feels connected when one is aware of family members' and friends' activities.

Figure 3.5 illustrates users rating on being connected to the community leader while Fig. 3.6 shows users' contribution in online social network. The users rated moderately on whether they felt they could contribute and share in their social network (2.99) (Fig. 3.6), they were a part of the online social network (2.88) (Fig. 3.7) and felt connected when they were aware of family members' and friends' activities (3.20) (Fig. 3.8). Those who rated highly (5 or 6) on the three items were basically the 18–24 year olds and 25–35 year olds.

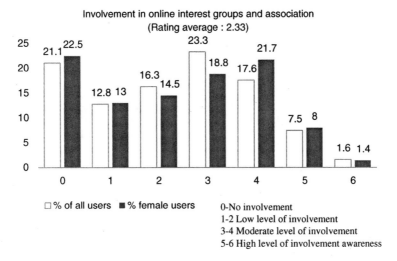

Fig. 3.4   Involvement in online interest groups and association

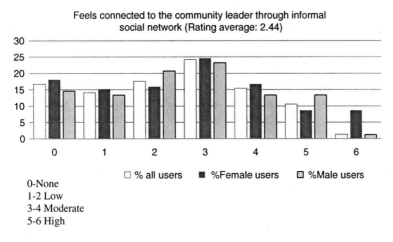

Fig. 3.5   Connected to the community leader

Users were also queried whether the utilization of RIC had brought positive or negative impact to their acquisition of information, communication with family and friends and meeting new people at the RIC or online. Despite a high percentage feeling the utilization of RIC had positively impacted them (see Table 3.5) on three measures of connectedness, the small percentage that conveyed negative impact on their 'meeting new acquaintance' is not to be ignored. This was described by both female and male RIC users. They were however, of the younger age group of 13–17 years. It is possible that the young users encountered negative experience when getting to know people online.

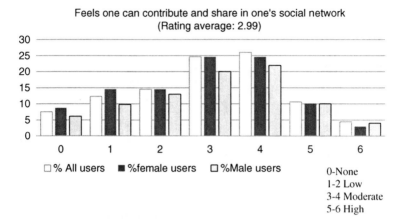

Fig. 3.6 Feels can contribute and share in a social network

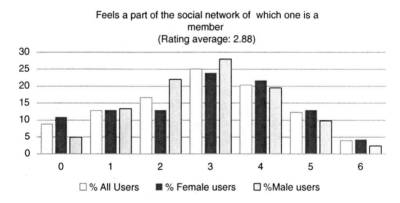

Fig. 3.7 Feels a part of a social network

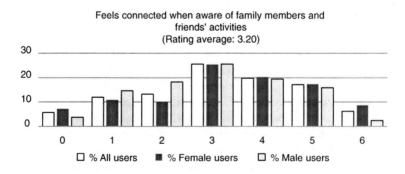

Fig. 3.8 Feels connected when aware of family members and friends' activities

Table 3.5 Impact of ICT access at the RIC

Impact	Strongly positive ++ (%)	Positive + (%)	0 (no impact)	Negative − (%)	Strongly negative − (%)
Access to information	60.7	30.4	3.3	0	0
Communication with family and friends	60.1	29.6	4.6	0	0
Meeting new acquaintances at the RIC or online	46.3	36.3	6.0	2.0	0.7

Connectedness to the leaders via social networking was not prevalent among the rural users. Of those who used the RIC for communication purposes, a small percentage reported accessing the Prime Minister' Facebook (16.4 %), State Minister's Facebook (8.4 %) and following the Prime Minister on Twitter account (4.2 %). Nonetheless, this signifies an interesting case of political leader connectedness. The users who were the state minister's Facebook friends were largely from three states ruled by the opposition party. They also accessed a daily newspaper online published by the party. The RIC thus has the potential to generate connectedness with the leaders and instill political awareness among the rural citizens.

3.5 Overall Level of Connectedness

Upon aggregation of all the items measuring the constructs of access, participation, involvement, relatedness and sense of belonging, a distribution of the respondents according to their level of connectedness is produced. Figure 3.9 shows a high percentage of the users with a moderate level of connectedness and a substantial percentage having low connectedness.

Upon closer scrutiny of the different RICs, high level of connectedness was found to be more apparent at the Marang RIC on the East Coast of Malaysia (24 % of the respondents charted a high level of connected) while more than half of the

Fig. 3.9 Overall level of connectedness

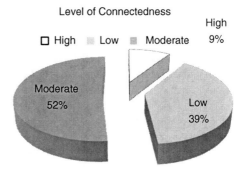

Level of Connectedness

□ High   Low   Moderate

High 9%

Moderate 52%

Low 39%

respondents from Rasa (52.9 %) reported to be lowly connected. These findings support the author's early conjecture that each RIC has its own uniqueness and warrants treatment as distinct cases. A brief discussion on the two abovementioned RICs follows.

3.5.1 Case of Connectedness: The Marang RIC

An email interview was conducted and a manager survey was administered to elicit information regarding Marang RIC. Marang RIC functions largely as an entrepreneur's centre. Users are actively involved in the social entrepreneur's club; a few users have started marketing their produce online. The venture necessitates a good knowledge of the internet, use of email and web publishing, thus resulting in a more proficient group who utilizes ICT to stay connected in business and to family and friends. Figure 3.10 illustrates Marang RIC users' connectedness.

Fig. 3.10 Level of connectedness of Marang RIC users

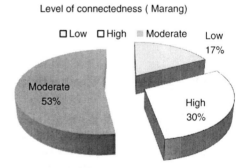

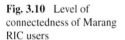

3.5.2 Case of Connectedness: The Rasa RIC

Rasa RIC on the other hand mimics a one stop community centre with users comprising youths, pensioners and housewives. Rasa RIC is among the few RICs that hosts users of different races, elderly users and users who were disable. The manager expressed the difficulty she faced in recruiting entrepreneurs who would like to be involved and trained at the RIC. The user demography was slightly different in Rasa where the races (Malay, Chinese and Indians) were equally distributed. Several middle aged women were interviewed in Rasa. They all showed interest to learn how to use the computer and the internet but had not reached a skilled level. According to the manager, training older adults to use ICT was a challenging feat as they would normally forget and lessons would have to be repeated. Thus the users' scores were low since they were not connected online (Fig. 3.11). They however, would meet at the RIC to get updates on each other's lives, visit the sick and take courses at a nearby college.

Fig. 3.11 Level of
connectedness of Rasa RIC
users

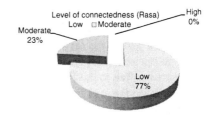

The levels of connectedness reported earlier took into account the connection made via online tools. The abovementioned cases of Marang and Rasa RICs highlighted different levels of connectedness that emerged out of ICT use at the RICs.

3.6   Further Discussion on Connectedness

The data elucidated several facets of connectedness that were apparent among the RIC users. Further analysis of interviews and qualitative responses from the survey confirmed these findings. Having access to information was the most frequent response given by the users who considered the ease of getting information as a way to stay connected. As reported in Alias et al. (forthcoming 2013),

> several users regarded it as being "connected to the world, the latest news and advances," and prevented them from being marginalized and "left out". Some phrased the access to information as a means to be connected to "external information", referring to events and occurrences outside their own community. "*Connecting beyond borders*" and "boundless *connectedness*" were among the expressions employed by the users. The phrases generate the idea of ubiquity and omnipresence; it allows the rural folks to stay connected to anybody, anywhere and at anytime. Another interesting observation was the connotation of being an informed person when connected to the world. A user implied "having access to the latest information and advances makes me a more knowledgeable person".

In addition, users were connected to others via emails and social networks. A user reported his access to ICT via RIC "enable me to make online social friends for the purpose of exchanging opinions on selected topics". This indicates a more than casual acquaintance. It is evident that RIC users are strengthening bridging ties and having the opportunity to connect beyond their community sphere. A few users proceeded to state social awareness as a result of having access to both online and activities at the RIC. A post office personnel spent his lunch hour staying connected to the various social groups and non governmental bodies as it "enhances social awareness" and "civic engagement". His case suggests the potential of ICT access in instigating social awareness.

Several users reported being connected to long lost friends and old friends via ICT utilization at the RIC. They also indicated feeling "close to friends". On a professional level, a number of users mentioned being connected to business associates and peers, resulting in a wider business network and providing potential for the ventures to thrive. Majority of the users however, have not reached the level of collaborating or co-creating.

Several users were also interviewed on the use of Government 2.0 tools such as the Prime Minister's Facebook. One particularly user contended that he chose not to be a part of the network because "it is not the Prime Minister who posted or reply to our posts; his staff does that". Others just did not find any reason to stay connected online to the Prime Minister. However, a user who was the village head saw the importance of having a Facebook account in order to stay connected to the state minister. In his case, the state minister maintains an active Facebook account and divulges information to his subordinates through the platform. As suggested earlier, the RIC has the potential to encourage connectedness to political leaders.

The abovementioned dimensions are incorporated in the framework of connectedness among rural internet center users presented earlier. What had escaped the attention of the authors earlier was the connectedness generated among business associates, clients and peers through the use of ICT and the RIC.

In general, RIC users were connected at a moderate level. The study also brought to light a number of observations.

1. The access to ICT via the utilization of RICs does impact the connectedness of rural Malaysians.
2. There were different levels of connectedness reported by the users.
3. Most users were connected at the lowest level of the typology (Fig. 3.5).
4. Preferred platform to connect varied according to the age group.
5. Older users tend to be connected through involvement in the RIC activities.
6. Younger users were more connected online.
7. Users who utilized the RIC to communicate with family members and friends living far away connected at a moderate level with family and friends.
8. Users who were entrepreneurs connected with their clients and business associates through utilization of ICT at the RIC.
9. Utility is a very important factor. Older users tend not to find the need to learn new web based tools to connect. They had little use for social networks; landlines and mobile phones were preferred in terms of personal touch and availability.
10. Users have yet to connect to community and top nation leaders via RIC utilization; however, the RIC has the potential to inculcate such connectedness.
11. There is no difference between the two genders in all aspects of connectedness
12. Connectedness varies according to RIC.

In terms of capacity development, the respondents in general perceived a personal level of empowerment. They agreed strongly on two aspects which were increased personal ICT-related skills and access to information and services but less on the ability to conduct personal online transactions after having access to ICT via RIC utilization. Increased self efficacy in which "individuals are able to engage in exercises that allow them to acquire and practice their skills in a non-threatening environment" (Amichai-Hamburger et al. 2008) was evident among women and older adults. In addition, there were indications of e-empowerment at the (1) interpersonal level where the respondents strengthened existing relationships and formed new ones and (2) group level where users reported finding similar others (e.g. business colleagues).

3.6.1 Typology of Connectedness

In the case of the Malaysian rural internet centers' users, connectedness is perceived to be of different levels. The pyramid in Fig. 3.12 signifies the levels of which the lower levels are more achievable as compared to the peak. The brief explores the lowest three levels; however the potential of the RIC to promote the upper levels is recognized.

Connectedness at a moderate degree and persistence of lower level connectedness were evident. Connectedness also varies according to RICs. Some RICS registered significantly higher level of connectedness compared to others.

Reasons for the moderate connectedness are believed to be related to the RIC utilization and other contributing factors as stated below.

Limited operating hours hinders participation and access..
Limited computer facility at the RICs is also a factor to consider. The highest number of working PCs reported is eight; otherwise, RICs make do with an average of three to four available PCs.
In relation to (b) is the lack of space allocated to some RICs. As commented by a user, "I have to squeeze in between and share the computer"
Restrictions are given by some managers on synchronous communication tools such as chats/instant messenger. Users come into use emails or contribute to social networking sites. Since responses are not real-time, users will have to come back another day. The communication flow is thus, disrupted as the above factors (a), (b) and (c) come into play.
Some users are not skilled or have not reached the level of IT competence.
Some users are apprehensive of the use of ICT to conduct transactions. Anxiety and lack of trust was evident especially among older adults who preferred human interaction.

The RIC embodies what technology is meant to be: (1) supportive, (2) generating personal and community development, (3) empowering and (4) linking people to others and the world. The previous chapter has brought to light the findings of a study done on Malaysian RIC users. Public access of ICT via RIC has been shown

Fig. 3.12 Typology of connectedness in the context of RIC users

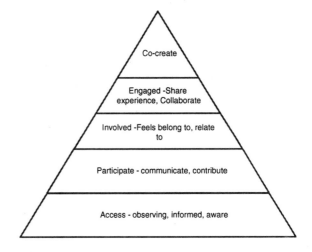

to impact users' personal capacity development and connectedness based on several measures such as access, participation, involvement, sense of belonging and sense of relatedness. Several reasons for moderate connectedness are discussed and the maintenance of RIC facility, its operational hours, its function and the role of the managers are highlighted.

References

Alias NA, Jamaludin H, Hashim S, Ismail IS, Suhaili N (2010) Theories of change and evaluation of Malaysian rural internet centers. Paper presented at the ICTD 2010 conference, London, 13–16 Dec 2010

Alias NA, Mohd Noor M, Proenza JP, Jamaludin H, Ismail IS, Hashim S (forthcoming 2013) Impact of public access to computers and the internet on the connectedness of rural Malaysians in ICT and Social Change: the impact of public access to computers and the internet, Amy Mahan Research Fellowship Program

Amichai-Hamburger Y, McKenna KYA, Tal S (2008) E-empowerment: empowerment by the internet. Comput Hum Behav 24(5):1776–1789. doi:10.1016/j.chb.2008.02.002

Afterword

The brief introduces the reader to the notion of connectedness in the context of rural communities whose members are less capable to acquire ICT in their own homes. A deliberation on the definition of connectedness and a brief account of ICT for development (ICT) are given beforehand to inform the readers of the many facets of connectedness and to frame the discussion within the parameters of rural connectedness. This brief then discusses access, participation, involvement, sense of relatedness, sense of belonging, and social connectedness in the light of rural users in Malaysia. The Rural Internet Center (RIC) operates as the point to connect. A description of the impact of ICT on personal capacity development is included to provide a clearer picture of what the users perceived. A typology of connectedness is generated to illustrate levels of connectedness evident from the study.

Despite lower levels of connectedness of the rural people, the potential of tele-centres or rural internet centers to propagate other dimensions of connectedness should not be ignored. In strategizing to do so, its function must not be limited to the provision of basic ICT training but to act as a 'server' to the community and as a communication gateway to the world outside the rural village. It is also an entryway for outsiders to connect to the village. As it is, RICs are scarcely known. A proper introduction to the outside communities is due. The RIC website therefore, plays a significant role in introducing the community to the world. Eco tourism, homestays and other pristine features unique to the village can be publicized to enhance business connectedness and to promote the village as a whole. Most villages have their own small business enterprises and unique services such as that of practitioners of alternative and traditional medicine that are sought by urban dwellers. The existing online network of RICs that has been established needs to be fostered to allow RICs to support each other. Establishing relevant content is thus mandatory.

The RIC should also be viewed as a platform for the community to stay informed of government initiatives. It is a mean to stay connected with the people. What has prevailed is the lack of connectedness between the rural communities and top leaders of the nation. While city dwellers access the government 2.0 tools, rural folks tend to be left behind. Connectivity has been taken care of. What is emerging is another facet to digital divide which is disconnectedness.

In terms of its relevance to the rural folks' education, the RICs could be utilized by teachers in the area to host educational contents that will support learning outside school hours. On another level, post secondary training institutes and higher education institutes could also be connected to the RIC to provide on-going courses, consultation and distance training in relevant fields. Distance learning is an especially relevant option for rural folks in the remote areas of East Malaysia who face transport problems and or are unable to leave home.

With respect to the recommendations given beforehand, it is imperative that the RIC website is linked to the ministry's and member of parliament's office. Business connectedness, government connectedness and social connectedness can be augmented towards the well being of the community.

RICs have impacted the rural communities in terms of quality, rather than quantity. Its benefits transpire over time. Thus in the light of cost effectiveness of government projects, it holds little interest and significance when reviewed with the number of users in mind.

Nevertheless, the study suggests that as a humble establishment, RIC has proven its ability to incite interest and awareness among rural users who have no or low ICT skills. Due to its attributes such as minimal charges, ongoing support, a readily available trainer, and convenient location, rural folks find the RIC a good place to start learning about ICT, to connect and to acquire skills that benefit many aspects of their lives. Some have gone ahead to buy their own computers and set up internet connections in their own homes but there are others who are still dependent on the RICs. Similar to a convenient store, the RIC is much needed entity but who goes in to "buy" what and at which hours depends on the needs of the community users. The RIC is not to be regarded as a school or as a training centre with a specific number of trainees churned out as an indicator of its performance. It is a support hub; a place to connect, and a center for ongoing skill acquisition and lifelong learning with someone to assist and to refer to. In the words of a user,

> The RIC is useful to senior citizens, housewives and adults because they are given less attention compared to students and youths. There is no other place to go to for these groups. The RIC indirectly helps these groups to be more confident in approaching ICT and learning it..become connected to the world....because the training is flexible and fulfills the learning needs of these groups...

CPSIA information can be obtained at www.ICGtesting.com
Printed in the USA
LVOW08s0619160713

343047LV00005BA/87/P